JULIE'S SIMPLE SOLUTIONS FOR:

CLEANING YOUR HOUSE IN *Minutes a Day*

BY JULIE SHORT

Published by:
FirstFruits Publishing
In Partnership with A Book's Mind
PO Box 272847
Fort Collins, CO 80527

Copyright © 2018
ISBN: 978-1-949563-10-8

Printed in the United States of America

TABLE OF CONTENTS

CLEANING CHARTS LOCATED IN THE BACK

JULIE'S SIMPLE SOLUTIONS FOR:
CLEANING YOUR HOUSE IN MINUTES A DAY

BY JULIE SHORT
A MUST READ INTRODUCTION

My son gave me a plaque when he was about 11 that had a picture of a cartoon "typical" housewife. Dressed in her flower print, no shape dress with a ruffled apron, hair up in curlers and a look that begged for someone to pluck her out of the pit she had fallen in and rescue her to a secluded island where dirt did not exist. The plaque read, "Cleaning the house while the kids are growing is like shoveling snow while it's still snowing!"

You don't have a lot of time. The time you do have, you certainly don't want to spend it all on cleaning. Sometimes it seems pointless anyway, right? How long does it really stay that way? While it may all seem in vain, we do want a clean house; for our sanity and for sanitary reasons. What if I told you that you can have a clean house in minutes a day? You may say, "Oh Julie, you don't know my family!" True, I don't, but they probably aren't too much different than mine.

When my husband and I first got married we were raising seven children together; mine, his and ours. This happens a lot more now days so I am sure there are many of you that can relate. We had a newborn, a two year old, 2 ½ , 4, 7, 8 and 10 year old. I had to learn how to work fast and efficiently.

There is no magic to what I am going to share with you; just some simple strategies and techniques. The main thing I want you to take from this book is a new way of thinking about cleaning. A way of thinking that can make you an excellent house keeper with less time and less effort. We are going to break your cleaning into bite sized projects and give you simple solutions for the sometimes overwhelming task of housework.

If you have a family, getting them involved with the suggestions from the Chapter "Make It Fun" will be helpful and rewarding for all, if you work it the right way. Perception is reality so if they start thinking this is going to be torture, it will be. If you can get excited about it, you can get them excited about it and teach them basic skills that will benefit them throughout their lives.

HOW TO USE THIS BOOK

There are a few ways you can use this book. Here are some options:

OPTION #1:

You can follow the Monday – Saturday daily routine at the back of the book. If you complete each day's list, you will have cleaned your entire house over the course of the week. Of course there are still monthly and seasonal chores but your basic cleaning will be complete and you can take Sunday off. Begin again on Monday to keep your house clean all the time.

OPTION #2:

You can look at the "TIMED" list at the back of the book and start deciding what needs to be done most when you have 5, 10, 15 or 20 minutes to spare. For instance, your meat is thawing in the microwave for dinner so you have 5 minutes. That is time to either unload the dishwasher or fold a load of laundry. Yes, it really only takes 5 minutes.

OPTION #3:

Use either one of the above methods to delegate chores among the other family members of your household to be completed. You can use the "10 Minute Blitz" referenced on page ? Which chores are calling your name the loudest? Take care of those first and foremost.

CHAPTER 1

BITE SIZED CLEANING

Cleaning your house will be so much easier when you learn to make that mountain of cleaning into a mole hill. You know that old saying, "How do you eat an elephant……one bite at a time." Your mind is such a powerful tool in everything you do. It will take some practice, but small cleaning in the course of your other activities will keep things looking good all the time and you won't feel like that is all you do! You will find that you don't need to set aside an entire day every week just for cleaning.

Here is just a quick example so you see it in action:

It's 6:00am and I am about to run upstairs to make sure everyone is awake and getting ready for the day. Before I run up the stairs I make a quick stop at the laundry room to grab the clean stack of towels from the previous day's laundry and an empty grocery store bag. When I get upstairs to check on everyone I put the towels away and empty any trash from the bathrooms into my empty bag. If I notice that the mirrors or sinks look dirty I grab the disinfecting wipes from under the sink and give everything a quick wipe down, throw the wipe into my little garbage bag and head downstairs to throw it in the big trashcan.

I am back downstairs by 6:06am. My kids make their own beds and bring their dirty clothes to the laundry room each day.

I start laundry first thing every morning and try to get it moved to the dryer and the second load started before we leave the house to take the kids to school. We always have, at the least, two loads of laundry each day. In the evening if I am thawing out dinner or waiting for the water to boil for some pasta, I go fold a load and move the 2nd to the dryer and fold it before bedtime (during a commercial break of my favorite show) and the kids take their stacks upstairs on their way to bed.

When you put away your laundry, pick up the empty hangers and any dirty clothes to be taken back to the laundry room. If your washer is empty, go ahead and put all of the darks or all of the whites in it. When it is full you can start a load.

When you climb out of bed, turn around and make it right then. It takes about one minute, throw pillows and all.

When you climb out of the shower, turn around and wipe it down with your towel after you have dried off. Use that towel to wipe your sink and counter top when you are finished getting ready. You can even use it on your mirror for spot cleaning.

Don't just put your dishes in the sink. It takes just a few more seconds to go ahead and rinse them and put them in the dishwasher. If each family member does this, the kitchen always looks good. If you are taking out the trash and it isn't completely full, take the bag over to the refrigerator and get rid of the take out that didn't get eaten or the broccoli that is going bad. You don't have to go through everything in the fridge, just grab the obvious and it just takes a few seconds.

All of these little ways of getting things done will add up to a cleaner house in less time. It is just a matter of you thinking about cleaning in a different way. See it as small jobs that can be done in minutes, rather than a big task. Yes, eventually you will have to clean the refrigerator out and wipe down the shelves but how much easier will it be since you have been doing a little bit here and there.

In Chapter 7 you will see how your vacuum clean can help you clean out your refrigerator, your toaster and many other things you haven't thought of using it for! You will learn ways to clean that may feel like you are CHEATING.

Have you ever noticed that mess begets mess? You don't make the bed. When you walk in and it's unmade, you through your clothes on it and leave your shoes all around it. Why wouldn't you? It's already a mess so there is no problem adding to it. But, if that bed is made up neat and tidy, you will be more likely to go put those clothes in the laundry and put your shoes in the closet to keep everything looking good. It works the same way in the kitchen; if there are already dishes sitting around what's the big deal of adding another one to the collection? If all is in order, you don't want to mess it up. Your family will catch on as well. We are all so influenced by one another.

I heard a woman on the radio talking about house cleaning and the fact that so many of us wait until we have the time to clean every nook and crevice before we do any of it. How many of us actually get the time to do it that way? That makes it so much harder and you end up with a dirty house the majority of the time, because most of us do not want to use the time we have for such a thing. This leads us to feeling guilty because we aren't wonder woman, makes us mad at our family because "why can't they just be neater?" and keeps our mind cluttered along with the house.

CHAPTER 2

GET A ROUTINE

Getting a routine for cleaning will help you stay ahead of the game and allow you to work your cleaning into your everyday life. It will also help you to clear your mind of the cleaning issue. Based on an average size home with three bedrooms and two bathroom, here is what needs to be done to keep a clean house:

DAILY

Dishes – 5 load or unload

Kitchen counters/sink - 5

Make beds – 1 minute per bed

Laundry - 5   minutes to start a load/ 1 minute to move it to the dryer/ 5 minutes to fold/hang

WEEKLY

Dusting - 15

Clean mirrors and glass - 10

Empty all trash cans - 5

Take trash out - 5

Sweep - 15

Mop - 15

Vacuum - 20

Microwave/Toaster/Coffee Maker - 5
Bathrooms – 15 each
Change Sheets – 5 each bed
Discard old items from refrigerator - 2

MONTLY

Ceiling fans and high corners - 5
Blinds, window sills and things hanging on walls - 20
Light fixtures - 15
Move furniture when vacuuming/under cushions as
well – additional 15
Wipe down baseboards, switch plate covers and doors - 20
Wipe down refrigerator - 10

EVERY FEW MONTHS

Wipe down doors and jambs - 15
Windows - 20
Vents covers - 15
Cabinet doors - 15
Oven - 10

Continually clean out closets and drawers of things that don't fit or may have missing buttons or stains that cannot be removed. Give away the appropriate items to charity. I keep a bag going all the time of "give away" items. If you do this every time you run across something that doesn't work for you, you won't have as much to do when its spring cleaning time. You can do the same thing with your children's toys and clothes. It is a great feeling knowing that someone else can benefit from the things you are not using and you are freeing yourself and your home of clutter.

Now that you have the ROUTINE of what needs to be done, how are you going to do it? I am sure you noticed the numbers to the right of each chore. That is the number of minutes this chore actually takes to complete. Breaking it down into the minutes will help you to either set aside a time to complete all the chores at once, or it will help you to see what you have time to complete or start, whichever the case may be, in the morning before you leave with the rest waiting for you when you return. This is explained further on the charts.

Of course, not every house has the same amount of traffic through it, and the sizes vary, but this will give you a ballpark idea of the time it takes to do household chores. These times are also based on maintenance style cleaning. If needed, you will want to do a thorough cleaning in the beginning and then begin the "Minutes a Day" way of cleaning to maintain. See the next chapter.

CHAPTER 3

TOP TO BOTTOM

$\mathcal{D}$epending on what shape your house is in currently, you may want or need to do a total deep clean before you begin the maintenance style of cleaning laid out in this book. Don't be afraid of the total deep clean. Remember, getting started is the hard part. A body in motion stays in motion and once you get started cleaning it will make you want to keep going.

Before you begin the cleaning of your house it would be beneficial if you would do a "cleaning out" of your house. By that, I mean going through closets and cabinets and getting rid of things that you do not need. This will help you enjoy what you do have and help others if you donate the excess to charity. Your house will be easier to clean without clutter. It doesn't mean you don't love your Great Aunt Edna just because you give away the jell-o mold shaped like Big Bird that she gave you. Stuff does not equal love! Stuff does not help you to honor the memory of a person. Stuff is just stuff so keep it in perspective. If you need it, (not if you MIGHT need it someday) keep it. If you don't, pass it on to someone who does.

So, now that you have cleared out all the junk, let's clean up! Cleaning top to bottom does work best if you can set aside an entire day. If that is not an option, you can break it into segments. You can opt to do this by completing a room top to bottom before moving on to the next or you can go through the entire house with each item before moving to the next.

I suggest completing a room before moving to the next if you have to break this into segments. If you have the entire day, going through the house with each item is more efficient.

Literally start at the top and work your way to the bottom throughout every area of the house.

Change air filters and vacuum or wipe down the vents
Clean any cob webs from the ceiling and walls. Check all corners.
Clean all ceiling fans and lights
Dust/clean all windows and wall hangings
Clean blinds and window sills
Clean all curtains and window treatments
Clean windows
Wipe down all cabinets/Oil if needed
Wipe down all counter tops
Clean all doors and door jambs
Clean all switch plate covers
Dust all furniture and knick knacks, any decorative items
Clean all bathrooms: Mirrors, sinks, countertops, tubs, showers, toilets
Wipe down baseboards
Sweep
Vacuum
Mop

You can refer to the sections of the book that give you tips on some products to make cleaning easier and the best ways to clean. Hopefully you have already cleaned out your drawers, closets and cabinets during your "clean out" so that you are starting with a clean slate. It will be helpful to hire someone to assist you with the top to bottom clean, if you have the opportunity. Plan on spending a minimum of $150, if you are going to hire outside help for this one time clean. You should be able to handle your maintenance cleaning from here on out.

CHAPTER 4

MAKE IT FUN

When I was growing up, there were 5 of us kids. We lived in a tiny town and a tiny house with one bathroom for 7 people to share. We converted the garage to make an additional bedroom but still had only the one bathroom. But, love grows best in little houses right! Believe it or not when you have a bigger space and a place for all your things it is easier to keep that space clean than a small space that you are trying to fit a lot in.

My mom always kept the house bottom clean, but with that many kids in that space, if we each left just one or two things lying around it made the whole house look cluttered. My mom had this little trick to get us involved with the cleaning without it seeming like torture even to my brothers.

We did a little thing called the "10 Minute Blitz". My mom would get us all together and set the timer for 10 minutes, reminding us of what a short amount of time that is. Everyone was supposed to clean and straighten for the entire 10 minutes with no potty breaks or drinks until the time was up. She promised if we worked diligently during the blitz then that is all we would have to do and not a minute more. So the time would begin and off we would go; putting away shoes, toys and laundry. We were wiping down counters, dusting, windows, mirrors, sweeping and vacuuming. When that timer went off ending our work, there were lots of whoops and clapping. At the end of the blitz everyone would meet up again and report to mom what all we had accomplished. She would brag on us for a job well done and gush over how great everything looked. It was like a game for us kids. We had the competition of who could get more done and the desire to receive the kudos from mom. We also had the motivation of knowing that if we slacked off during the 10 minutes, she would add time and be very disappointed. Just think about it, six of us working for 10 minutes, is equal to a solid hour of cleaning! I believe this game helped me look at housework in a different way. It made me see it could be fun and rewarding and it didn't have to be a huge daunting task.

I hope that this book will help you break up your task into small do-able list that you can accomplish in the amount of time you used to take to complain about having to do it.

Getting your family involved will definitely make things easier on you and there is a benefit for them as well. Letting them know that you are all a team and it takes all of you to be successful sounds good until they realize it means real work for them. Reality stinks sometimes. It doesn't mean they don't love you, it just means we all tend to look out for our own interest and they just aren't that interested in a clean house. I am not opposed to allowance for helping with chores but each person picking up after themselves is something they should do without being paid. Your children also need to know that the less time you have to spend on the house, the more time you will have to play with them, help them with projects or take trips. Your husband might be a little more helpful if he realizes how much you appreciate him helping you make the bed or clear the table. Telling him how much you appreciate his help instead of, "It's about time you started doing something around here!" will ensure that you get help more often. He will also start to notice that you have some extra time to sit with him on the couch and that you aren't so completely worn out when it's time for bed.

Getting everyone involved in the "top to bottom" cleaning can be a great way to make the family aware that some changes are being made and make it a positive thing. If everyone gets involved, you could set aside a Saturday for the big clean and promise a night out at the movies as a reward. This will give everyone ownership in the "clean" house and help them to want to keep it that way in minutes a day.

Simple acts such as loading your dishes as soon as you are finished eating, instead of just setting them in the sink, really make a big difference with very little effort. You are already handling the dish so take the extra 5 seconds to put it in the dishwasher. This also works for taking off your dirty clothes and throwing them in the hamper instead of in the floor. Take them off near the hamper and you won't have to even think about it as being an extra step. Make it easy and make it handy to be neat.

Also realize your version of clean and your kids version of clean probably differ, vastly. When you ask if their room is clean and you get a cheerful "Yes!", you might want to specify, "Is it my version of clean?".

Teach your kids this simple step. Before you leave a room, simply turn around and look. Is everything in place?

CHAPTER 5

NO TIME LIKE THE PRESENT

Today is the day, now is the time. Don't wait until you have the whole day open before you pick up a rag or a cleaning product. I give an example in this book of incorporating wiping down bathroom, emptying trashcans and putting away laundry into waking the kids up for school. Start looking for ways you can sneak in some cleaning while you are on your way to do something else or while you are waiting, even if it is only a minute. You can make a bed in one minute.

What chores are calling your name? Do you notice crumbs in the kitchen floor every time you walk through the house? Get the broom and sweep up the crumbs. You don't have to make a big deal out of it. You don't have to go corner to corner on the kitchen and plan on mopping as well. Just get the broom and take a minute to get up the crumbs or take five minutes and sweep the entire kitchen.

Maybe you notice that the front door needs to be cleaned. On your way out the door grab some paper towels, spray them with cleaner and wipe down that door as your leaving. It only takes a minute. It may take some getting used to for you to start thinking about your cleaning in this way but it is going to make your life much easier.

One of my tricks is to try and make every move dual purpose. I don't ever run up the stairs without taking something from downstairs that needs to be put away, whether its laundry, toys or extra toilet paper and shampoo. I keep a couple of empty grocery sacks under my bathroom sink so that I can empty my bathroom trash into them and then carry it to the big trashcan when I take my dirty clothes to the laundry room. It may seem like such a small thing but that is one less trip I will have to make and it makes my bathroom look neater.

One thing that will help you with taking care of what needs to be done immediately is having the best and most convenient cleaning products handy. Here are a few of my favorites and how they make life easier.

The right equipment or proper tools is said to be the thing that separates professionals from amateurs. The right products for cleaning can help make it fun and a whole lot easier. They will help you work smart, not hard.

Lysol Bathroom Wipes – These little wipes are great to keep under every bathroom sink in the house. When you see that the sink, countertops, toilet or tub needs a quick wipe down, just grab a couple and go to work. In just a few minutes your bathroom will be shining and clean with very little effort from you.

Windex Wipes – Just like the wipes mentioned above, these are great under every sink for making your mirrors shine and your faucets as well.

Clorox Wipes – Great to have in the kitchen and for wiping down doors and switch plate covers.

I do not do the serious cleaning with the wipes. They are too expensive to use in that way and there are other products I like for the deep down cleaning.

Spray Way – This window cleaner can cut through all kinds of dirt and grime. I buy mine at Sam's Club but I have seen it in the regular grocery stores as well. I also use it on my kitchen sink, faucet and countertops sometimes.

Swiffer Duster w/ the extendable pole – Oh my goodness this thing is great! Dusting has always been at the bottom of my list of things I like to do because I always felt like I couldn't really get all the dust and at 5'4 I have a hard time reaching so many things that need to be dusted. This little tool makes it all better and I don't even complain about it anymore. I actually get excited about finding new ways to use it like extending the pole and dusting baseboards without having to bend over. I can do the pictures hanging on the wall and reach most of my light fixture without having to pull out the ladder or step stool. I can also get the legs of tables without having to get under the table. This is also great for stairs and going around the railing.

Dow Scrubbing Bubbles – I love this product. You can see exactly where you have sprayed. I like the smell and no scrubbing is necessary. They really do the work for you. I spray down bathroom counter tops/sinks/tub/shower and toilet with this. I have also used it on the inside of microwave when stuff is hard to scrub off.

Swiffer Wet Jet – The smell of the cleaning solution will make your entire house smell clean. I like the fact that I can go straight from tile to wood without having to change products. The head swivels nicely and is great for getting around the sides of the toilet up close.

Clorox Clean Up – Great to have in the kitchen for disinfecting after certain food items. An all around good cleaner when you don't know what else to use. Just remember it is a bleach so use your white rags and don't get it on your clothes or carpets.

Comet Cleaner – The best thing I have found for scrubbing stains out of a stainless steel sink especially around the drain and disposal. Very cost effective. I would not use it on a daily basis because it is pretty abrasive.

Of course you will need to make sure these products are safe for your surfaces before using any of them. There are many good products on the market if you just look. They smell great and are packaged for convenience and efficiency. Make sure you have plenty of products on hand. If possible, keep stock under every sink with some extra rags or paper towels so that it is always handy for quick touch ups.

CHAPTER 6

READY FOR ANYTHING

If you're old enough to be reading this book you have probably already learned that life can be very unexpected. Our routines are always being interrupted and that is not necessarily a bad thing, it helps keep things exciting. Having your house clean at all times (that doesn't mean perfect, but basically in order) will help you keep your sanity when the unexpected does occur.

I know I can't be the only one who has friends and neighbors just drop by sometimes. Family has been known to pop in without notice before as well. Personally, I do not mind the surprise visits and I know part of the reason is because my house is usually in order. I do not have to panic or make excuses for how things look.

How about vacation time? Yes, you plan your vacation but how many of us are scurrying around getting the house in order when we should be finding the perfect earrings to go with that cute little dress we want to wear for the special dinner planned on the trip? There will always be last minute things that need to be done to your house but if you are staying on top of the cleaning in minutes a day, you will have more time to concentrate on the fun you are about to have.

Births, deaths and unexpected illnesses are a part of this life and whether it's happening under your roof or with friends or relatives. The last thing you want to worry about during these occasions is your house being a wreck. You may end up with company staying in your home or you may have to be away. Either way, you want to have your house in order for your peace of mind.

CHAPTER 7

TIME STEALERS

We all have 24 hours each day, none of us get more and none of us get any less. What are you doing with yours? Well if you are the average American, you spend 10 – 12 of those 24 hours dealing with work. Getting ready for, traveling to and from, lunch, breaks and your actual working hours take up a lot of your time. If you are able to sleep for 8 full hours, you are now down to 4 – 6 hours left. Let's say you work out for 1 hour and you have to get some kind of breakfast together for the family, pack lunches and don't forget about dinner. I know…..you're tired just reading this! You might have 3 hours left for homework, baseball practice and your favorite show.

You are probably wondering how you get anything done with that kind of schedule. It is pretty amazing, the things you can accomplish in a day. My mom has always said, "If you want something done, give it to a busy person." You are like a locomotive, you get moving and you can cover a lot of ground fast. It's when you get side tracked that you start to feel like everything is piling up and there is going to be a derailment.

Some of the things that might be getting you off track and stealing your time are:

Emails – Wow these things seem to multiply faster than gray hairs when your kids get their driver's licenses. Yes, some of them are important, some are inspiring and some of them are just irritating. Set aside a certain time and a time limit to go through your emails. If you have 10 minutes and that doesn't look like it will be enough time, just deal with the important issues and save all of the inspiration and irritation for another day. If you have friends that forward you <u>everything</u>, give yourself the freedom to delete without reading. I give you permission! Oh don't think I forgot about Facebook, My Space and Twitter either! You can waste an entire afternoon on these things. They aren't bad but you need to put some limits on your time here as well.

Phone Calls from friends – There are lots of task you can perform while you are on the phone. In fact, it can make your work go faster in some cases. But, if you feel like you need to sit down and focus on the conversation then it needs to wait until you are free. Of course if there is a crisis that would be an exception but some of us have friends that are always in "crisis". You have to prioritize and get the "have to" stuff done first to keep your own sanity. There is nothing wrong with letting your friends know you are available after 8:00pm, for instance, or that you will give them a call back later.

TV – There is very little on television that will truly benefit you. If you want to watch for pure entertainment then record your show to be watched when you have time and you can fast forward thru the commercials so that it takes less time or you can watch your show but jump up during the commercials to get some of your stuff done.

Unimportant task – I am one of the worst about getting involved in some little detailed cleaning job when I need to be taking care of the basics. I might go to grab the cleaning products under the sink and decide it needs to be organized under there and spend the next bit of time doing that instead of wiping down the bathrooms like I was planning. Take care of the basic general cleaning and then go back and do the detailed things when the other is completed. You can make time for all of the things that are important to you. Time can work for you when you prioritize and set some limits so that it doesn't get away from you.

CHAPTER 8

THE BEST WAY TO..........

Maybe I should write a book called "101 Ways to Use Your Vacuum Cleaner". My vacuum cleaner is such an important tool in keeping the house looking good. Of course, I vacuum the carpets with it, but it also works great on tile and wood floors. When I hook up the hose, the cleaning possibilities are endless. It makes cleaning so easy I almost feel like I'm cheating. The hose extends to far reaching and has an attachment with a very slim end to get into cracks and crevices where no man has gone before!

Check out some of the ways I cheat:

Baseboards

Under cabinet edges

Under the cushions and between the seams

Counter tops

Stove top and into vent/filter area

Microwave – if its dry bits

Toaster – inside slots, crumb trays and underneath

Refrigerator – inside drawers and on shelves

Spice cabinet – where the salt and pepper may have fallen over, etc.

Vent Covers

Inside cabinet drawers of kitchen and bathrooms

Window sill and blinds

Curtains and window treatments
Fake greenery
Shoe basket
Pantry shelves
On walls and in corners for cob webs
Tops of door jambs
Tops of wall hangings and decorations, if possible, depending on size and style

My vacuum also has attachments for shampooing the carpets, painting a room or blowing leaves.

I know some of the following sections may seem simple or obvious to some of you but there are many who do not have any cleaning experience so we will start from scratch. If I know any tricks for the particular task, they are included.

Sweep the floor –

Option 1 – If you have a vacuum cleaner that works on hard surface floors, this makes it easy and you can use the hose to get under the edges if needed.

Option 2 – The broom is still your best option for quick clean ups and when you don't want to get the vacuum out. First of all, you need a good quality broom and an even better dust pan. It is so frustrating to just be moving the dirt around with cheap tools. Start at the farthest corner of the room and begin sweeping from the edge. Work on an area of about a 6 foot out and across at a time, sweeping towards yourself. Make small piles of dirt for each area. After you get a few little piles, scoop them into the dust pan and empty the contents into the trash. Repeat until all areas are dirt free and all piles are transferred to the trash.

Vacuum – Start at one end of the house, at the farthest corner of the room and work your way backwards across the carpets so that you do not leave your own foot prints on your freshly cleaned floors. I have Berber carpet so it is not an issue for me.

No lovely lines in the carpet but no foot prints either. You can refer to the prior list for additional vacuuming options.

Mop – Make sure that you have vacuumed or swept the area very well before you begin to mop or you will be making mud. I use the Swiffer Wet Jet and it makes mopping so easy. No mixing and no measuring needed. Just attach a clean pad to the bottom and start at the farthest point of the room or area and work your way backwards out of the room. Spray the product as needed and change out the pad as needed. The cleaner works great on my tile and hardwood floors so I do not have to switch products for the different areas. It smells wonderful too!

If you are using a traditional mop, just make sure that you have squeezed all excess liquid before you begin mopping and rinse regularly, depending on the condition of the floors you are cleaning. You can mix some products in your bucket of water and there are some products you spray onto the floor as you go. Make sure the products you use are safe for your flooring surfaces. If your floor feels a little "tacky" when you are finished it probably just means you need a little less product and a little more water in the mix.

Dusting – The Swiffer Duster is a great tool. I have the extendable pole and it allows me to reach things I could not with a traditional feather duster or a rag. This product is also great because you do not have to use a spray and it works on glass and wood. It grabs the dust and you don't just move dirt around. Now there are times and certain pieces of furniture for which I like to use furniture polish. Most of the time, less is better with the spray. Use a cleaning rag that is safe for your wood and is very absorbent. Make sure you switch to a fresh rag if yours starts to get dirty. Put the product on the rag instead of directly on the furniture. The furniture oil is my favorite for my cabinet doors. It makes the whole room shine. Whatever you're dusting, start high and work your way down.

Counter tops – A damp rag is usually all that is needed. I have black counter tops so I usually have a damp rag in one hand and a dry one in the other so that no water spots are left behind. Go under your canister and decorations on those counter tops, it makes a difference especially if you get lots of natural sunlight in your room. You don't have to make it a big deal when you move your stuff to go under it. Just pick it up, wipe and put it back down or slide it to the side, wipe and return. Wipe any crumbs into your hand and throw them in the trash so that the floors stay nice.

Microwave – A damp cloth is the best for a quick wipe down. I have used the Dow scrubbing bubbles on "stuck on" stuff. I have also put ½ a lemon in a bowl of water and put it in the microwave for about 2 minutes and it loosens everything up to make the wipe down easy. Be careful when you take the bowl out, it will be hot.

Bathrooms – Spray the tub, shower, toilet, sinks and countertops with Dow Scrubbing Bubbles. Spray your mirrors and faucets with Sprayway. Use paper towels and clean the mirrors, then glass shower doors and finish up with the faucets. If your paper towel is still ok wipe out the sinks and do the counter tops before you move on to the tub. The paper towels I use are a little rough so they are great for scrubbing. I also have some great cleaning rags that I use. Make sure you don't put any fabric softener in with your cleaning rags and you will have to do a little less scrubbing. The shower is next and lastly the toilet. Make sure you do the entire toilet; wipe the top of the tank, the tank, around the outside of the bowl and the base. Then the lid, seat and under the seat. Use a brush for the inside. No one should have to go there!

Glass/Mirrors – Using a dry rag is the best way to make sure you don't have streaks in your work. If yours starts to get damp, get another one. I like SprayWay because if cuts through gunk and it doesn't run very quickly. I use Windex also. I have both under my kitchen sink. Windex has the disposable wipes that make bathroom touch ups easy. Again, start at the top and work your way down, going all the way to the edges. Look at it from a couple of different angles to make sure you got all the spots and streaks.

Kitchen Sink/Disposal – I have a stainless steel sink and it usually looks good if I just spray it with the Sprayway and wipe it down. If it starts getting some food stains, a little Ajax sprinkled in and scrub it down with a rag. Rinse it and dry it out to make it look perfect. I don't use the Ajax everyday because I think it can be a little harsh. Throw a slice of lemon or the lime from your cherry limeade down the disposal ever now and then to clean it up. Make sure you wipe down the outer edges of the sink and the back of the sink, where the scrubber and soap sit. Details make the difference between just looking ok and looking polished.

Clean the oven – I currently have a self cleaning oven and it is awesome. I set it to self clean, wait the allotted time and simple wipe out (or vacuum) the crumbs when it's done. I haven't always been so lucky but the oven cleaners these days work very well. Make sure you follow the directions exactly and move your trash can close by so you can wipe and shake your rag out regularly.

Make a Bed – Make sure your sheets are smooth; they don't have to be perfect. Pull up the comforter or quilt and smooth out the wrinkles! Put the pillows on with case openings facing the center of the bed so that the outer edges look smooth. Add decorative pillows and you are good to go in about one minute.

Clean your blinds and window sills – Vacuum or wipe out any dust, dead insects or debris. You can vacuum the blinds quickly by using the attachment that has a brush type end. Turn the blinds completely one direction and vacuum before turning the other direction to vacuum. If needed, use a damp cloth to wipe down. The Swiffer

Duster can also be used for this and is great at getting in between the individual slats.

Clean your ceiling fans – The Swiffer Duster can be used in many cases and is especially good for cleaning the lights of the fan. I also have a tool specifically for ceiling fans that has an oblong brush with a hole in the middle that fits the blade so that top, bottom and sides are cleaned at once. This works well if it has been awhile and the dirt is a little more stubborn.

Load the dishwasher – Face all your plates and bowls the same direction. Put all flatware in handle end first so that they spread out at the top instead of lying against each other where parts can get missed. Make sure you do not block any moving parts or water flow. Put all sharp knives together and put them in point end first so that you do not accidentally grab them when unloading. Do not overload your dishwasher. Remember, the more organized you are when loading, the more you can fit and not have to hand wash!

TIMED CHART

PICK ONE OF THE FOLLOWING CHORES BASED ON HOW MUCH TIME YOU HAVE AND WHAT IS MOST NEEDED.

5 MINUTES

Each of these chores can be completed in 5 minutes or less.

*Unload the dishwasher
*Load the dishwasher
*Sweep the kitchen
*Sweep the bathroom
*Mop a room
*Clean the microwave

*Empty all the trash cans
*Take the trash out
*Scrub a toilet
*Clean the tub
*Vacuum a room
*Clean sink/disposal

*Windex the bathroom mirror/glass
*Start a load of laundry
*Move laundry from washer to dryer (about 1 minute)
*Fold\Hang a load of laundry   *Change the sheets on a bed
*Wipe down the shower   *Make the bed (about 1 minute)
*Wipe down the kitchen counters/sinks

10 MINUTES

Each of these chores can be completed in about 10 minutes.

*Clean out the refrigerator   *Organize your pantry

*Organize a cabinet of items   *Wipe down all switch plate covers

*Clean the oven (after timed cleaning with product or self cleaning oven)

*Put away the laundry   *Sweep your porches

15 MINUTES

Each of these chores can be completed in about 15 minutes.

*Dust all furniture   *Vacuum all baseboards with attachment

*Clean all mirrors   *Oil kitchen cabinets

20 MINUTES

Each of these chores can be completed in about 20 minutes.

*Vacuum a 1-story house   *Mop all floors

*Clean the blinds   *Vacuum curtains/window treatments

MONTHLY CHART

MONDAY	TUESDAY	WEDNESDAY	THURSDAY	FRIDAY	SATURDAY
1 MAKE BEDS START LAUNDRY MOVE LAUNDRY TO DRYER FOLD/HANG LAUNDRY UNLOAD DISHWASHER LOAD DISHWASHER WIPE DOWN KITCHEN COUNTERS/SINK 35 Minutes	**2** MAKE BEDS START LAUNDRY MOVE LAUNDRY TO DRYER FOLD/HANG LAUNDRY UNLOAD DISHWASHER LOAD DISHWASHER WIPE DOWN KITCHEN COUNTERS/SINK SWEEP/MOP KITCHEN EMPTY TRASHCANS TAKE TRASH OUT 55 Minutes	**3** MAKE BEDS START LAUNDRY MOVE LAUNDRY TO DRYER FOLD/HANG LAUNDRY UNLOAD DISHWASHER LOAD DISHWASHER WIPE DOWN KITCHEN COUNTERS/SINK CLEAN 1 BATHROOM 55 Minutes	**4** MAKE BEDS START LAUNDRY MOVE LAUNDRY TO DRYER FOLD/HANG LAUNDRY UNLOAD DISHWASHER LOAD DISHWASHER WIPE DOWN KITCHEN COUNTERS/SINK CLEAN MICROWAVE CLEAN 1 BATHROOM 60 Minutes	**5** MAKE BEDS START LAUNDRY MOVE LAUNDRY TO DRYER FOLD/HANG LAUNDRY UNLOAD DISHWASHER LOAD DISHWASHER WIPE DOWN KITCHEN COUNTERS/SINK DUST FURNITURE CLEAN FRIDGE 65 Minutes	**6** MAKE BEDS START LAUNDRY MOVE LAUNDRY TO DRYER FOLD/HANG LAUNDRY UNLOAD DISHWASHER LOAD DISHWASHER WIPE DOWN KITCHEN COUNTERS/SINK VACUUM HOUSE AND MOVE FURNITURE 65 Minutes
8 MAKE BEDS START LAUNDRY MOVE LAUNDRY TO DRYER FOLD/HANG LAUNDRY UNLOAD DISHWASHER LOAD DISHWASHER WIPE DOWN KITCHEN COUNTERS/SINK CLEAN CEILING FANS 55 Minutes	**9** MAKE BEDS START LAUNDRY MOVE LAUNDRY TO DRYER FOLD/HANG LAUNDRY UNLOAD DISHWASHER LOAD DISHWASHER WIPE DOWN KITCHEN COUNTERS/SINK 55 Minutes	**10** MAKE BEDS START LAUNDRY MOVE LAUNDRY TO DRYER FOLD/HANG LAUNDRY UNLOAD DISHWASHER LOAD DISHWASHER WIPE DOWN KITCHEN COUNTERS/SINK CLEAN 1 BATHROOM 55 Minutes	**11** MAKE BEDS START LAUNDRY MOVE LAUNDRY TO DRYER FOLD/HANG LAUNDRY UNLOAD DISHWASHER LOAD DISHWASHER WIPE DOWN KITCHEN COUNTERS/SINK CLEAN MICROWAVE CLEAN 1 BATHROOM 60 Minutes	**12** MAKE BEDS START LAUNDRY MOVE LAUNDRY TO DRYER FOLD/HANG LAUNDRY UNLOAD DISHWASHER LOAD DISHWASHER WIPE DOWN KITCHEN COUNTERS/SINK DUST FURNITURE CLEAN FRIDGE 65 Minutes	**13** MAKE BEDS START LAUNDRY MOVE LAUNDRY TO DRYER FOLD/HANG LAUNDRY UNLOAD DISHWASHER LOAD DISHWASHER WIPE DOWN KITCHEN COUNTERS/SINK VACUUM HOUSE AND GO UNDER CUSHIONS 65 Minutes

15	16	17	18	19	20
MAKE BEDS START LAUNDRY MOVE LAUNDRY TO DRYER FOLD/HANG LAUNDRY UNLOAD DISHWASHER LOAD DISHWASHER WIPE DOWN KITCHEN COUNTERS/SINK CLEAN THE BLINDS 55 Minutes	MAKE BEDS START LAUNDRY MOVE LAUNDRY TO DRYER FOLD/HANG LAUNDRY UNLOAD DISHWASHER LOAD DISHWASHER WIPE DOWN KITCHEN COUNTERS/SINK 55 Minutes	MAKE BEDS START LAUNDRY MOVE LAUNDRY TO DRYER FOLD/HANG LAUNDRY UNLOAD DISHWASHER LOAD DISHWASHER WIPE DOWN KITCHEN COUNTERS/SINK CLEAN 1 BATHROOM 55 Minutes	MAKE BEDS START LAUNDRY MOVE LAUNDRY TO DRYER FOLD/HANG LAUNDRY UNLOAD DISHWASHER LOAD DISHWASHER WIPE DOWN KITCHEN COUNTERS/SINK CLEAN MICROWAVE CLEAN 1 BATHROOM 60 Minutes	MAKE BEDS START LAUNDRY MOVE LAUNDRY TO DRYER FOLD/HANG LAUNDRY UNLOAD DISHWASHER LOAD DISHWASHER WIPE DOWN KITCHEN COUNTERS/SINK DUST FURNITURE CLEAN FRIDGE 65 Minutes	MAKE BEDS START LAUNDRY MOVE LAUNDRY TO DRYER FOLD/HANG LAUNDRY UNLOAD DISHWASHER LOAD DISHWASHER WIPE DOWN KITCHEN COUNTERS/SINK DUST CHANDELIERS AND LIGHTS VACUUM HOUSE 55 Minutes

22	23	24	25	26	27
MAKE BEDS START LAUNDRY MOVE LAUNDRY TO DRYER FOLD/HANG LAUNDRY UNLOAD DISHWASHER LOAD DISHWASHER WIPE DOWN KITCHEN COUNTERS/SINK WIPE DOWN BASEBOARDS AND SWITCH PLATE COVERS 55 Minutes	MAKE BEDS START LAUNDRY MOVE LAUNDRY TO DRYER FOLD/HANG LAUNDRY UNLOAD DISHWASHER LOAD DISHWASHER WIPE DOWN KITCHEN COUNTERS/SINK 55 Minutes	MAKE BEDS START LAUNDRY MOVE LAUNDRY TO DRYER FOLD/HANG LAUNDRY UNLOAD DISHWASHER LOAD DISHWASHER WIPE DOWN KITCHEN COUNTERS/SINK CLEAN 1 BATHROOM 55 Minutes	MAKE BEDS START LAUNDRY MOVE LAUNDRY TO DRYER FOLD/HANG LAUNDRY UNLOAD DISHWASHER LOAD DISHWASHER WIPE DOWN KITCHEN COUNTERS/SINK CLEAN MICROWAVE CLEAN 1 BATHROOM 60 Minutes	MAKE BEDS START LAUNDRY MOVE LAUNDRY TO DRYER FOLD/HANG LAUNDRY UNLOAD DISHWASHER LOAD DISHWASHER WIPE DOWN KITCHEN COUNTERS/SINK DUST FURNITURE CLEAN FRIDGE 65 Minutes	MAKE BEDS START LAUNDRY MOVE LAUNDRY TO DRYER FOLD/HANG LAUNDRY UNLOAD DISHWASHER LOAD DISHWASHER WIPE DOWN KITCHEN COUNTERS/SINK VACUUM HOUSE 55 Minutes

All times are approximate. We don't all fit in a neat little box but it will certainly give you an idea of how long it should be taking. You will see that taking care of things on a daily basis makes the chores much more manageable. Following this chart will have your house looking great every day and you will have completed a thorough cleaning by the end of the 4 week period. There will still be seasonal things that need to be completed but this will get your basic cleaning knocked out in less than an hour on most days!

HAPPY CLEANING!!!!

ABOUT THE AUTHOR

Julie Short has been married to husband Stoney since 1997. Julie is currently working on a series of books known as Julie's Simple Solutions, some of those titles include; A Good Marriage, Cooking In Minutes A Day, Fitness In Minutes A Day, The Truth About God and more.

Stoney

Julie